I0448894

June 2013

ARMY INDUSTRIAL OPERATIONS

Budgeting and Management of Carryover Could Be Improved

GAO-13-499

June 2013

ARMY INDUSTRIAL OPERATIONS

Budgeting and Management of Carryover Could Be Improved

Highlights of GAO-13-499, a report to congressional requesters

Why GAO Did This Study

The 13 Army Industrial Operations activities support combat readiness by providing depot maintenance and ordnance services to keep Army units operating worldwide. To the extent that Industrial Operations does not complete work at year-end, the work and related funding will be carried over into the next fiscal year. Carryover is the reported dollar value of work that has been ordered and funded by customers but not completed by Industrial Operations at the end of the fiscal year. As requested, GAO reviewed issues related to Army Industrial Operations' carryover. GAO's objectives were to determine whether, and to what extent, Army Industrial Operations' (1) actual carryover exceeded allowable carryover for fiscal years 2006 through 2012; (2) budget information on carryover approximated actual information for fiscal years 2006 through 2012, and if not, whether the Army took actions to align the two; and (3) carryover increased during fiscal years 2011 and 2012 and causes for the carryover. To address these objectives, GAO reviewed relevant carryover guidance, analyzed carryover and related data for Industrial Operations, and interviewed Army officials.

What GAO Recommends

GAO is making three recommendations to the Department of Defense (DOD) that are aimed at implementing the planned actions identified by the Army's working group to improve the budgeting and management of carryover. DOD concurred with GAO's recommendations and cited related actions planned or under way.

View GAO-13-499. For more information, contact Asif A. Khan at (202) 512-9869 or khana@gao.gov.

What GAO Found

From fiscal years 2006 through 2012, Army's Industrial Operations' actual carryover was under the allowable amounts in 5 of the 7 fiscal years. However, carryover more than doubled during that period, reaching a high of $5.8 billion in fiscal year 2011. Army officials stated that fiscal year 2011 was an abnormal year because Industrial Operations (1) received more orders than it had ever received—$7.5 billion in new orders—and (2) implemented a system called the Logistics Modernization Program (LMP) that changed the business rules for recognizing revenue and therefore resulted in carryover being higher than it would have been under the prior system. Army officials anticipate carryover decreasing in fiscal year 2013. According to the Army fiscal year 2014 budget, the Army expects carryover to be under $4 billion at the end of fiscal year 2013.

Industrial Operations' New Orders, Revenue, Carryover, and Months of Carryover
Dollars in millions

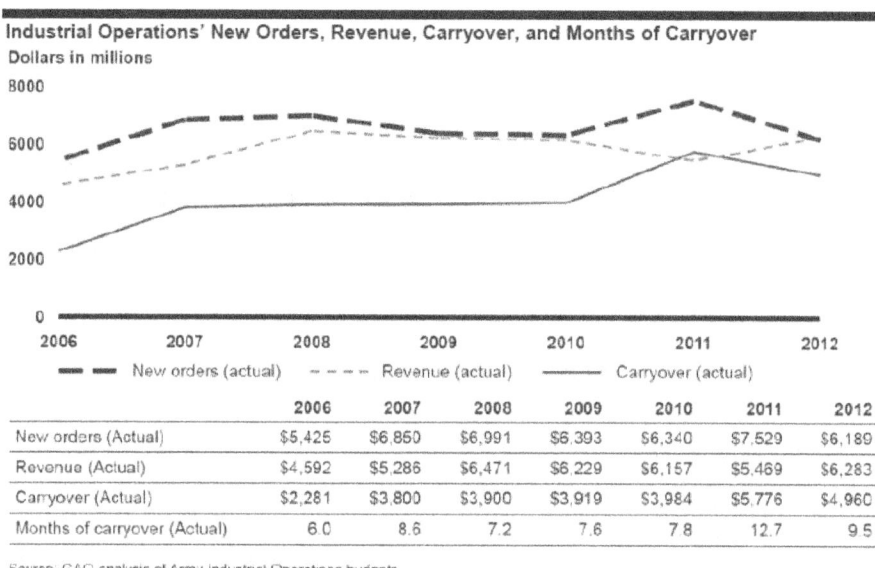

	2006	2007	2008	2009	2010	2011	2012
New orders (Actual)	$5,425	$6,850	$6,991	$6,393	$6,340	$7,529	$6,189
Revenue (Actual)	$4,592	$5,286	$6,471	$6,229	$6,157	$5,469	$6,283
Carryover (Actual)	$2,281	$3,800	$3,900	$3,919	$3,984	$5,776	$4,960
Months of carryover (Actual)	6.0	8.6	7.2	7.6	7.8	12.7	9.5

Source: GAO analysis of Army Industrial Operations budgets.

The Army's budget estimates for carryover were less than the actual carryover amounts each year beginning in fiscal year 2006—at least $1.1 billion each year. GAO's analysis showed that the actual amounts of carryover exceeded budgeted amounts primarily because (1) the Army underestimated new orders to be received from customers for all 7 years reviewed, particularly with respect to procurement funded orders, and (2) for fiscal year 2011, Industrial Operations performed over $1 billion less work than budgeted because Army officials were unaware of the impact that LMP would have on revenue when developing the fiscal year 2011 budget. The Army is taking actions intended to better align the customers' budgets with Industrial Operations' budgets.

Industrial Operations' carryover grew significantly in fiscal years 2011 and 2012 to represent about 12.7 and 9.5 months of work, respectively. GAO found three causes for the carryover: (1) the scope of requested work was not well defined, (2) parts were not available to perform the work, and (3) revenue recognition business rules were changed as part of the implementation of LMP. The Army formed a working group in April 2012 that identified actions to help reduce carryover. However, these actions have not been implemented and no timetable for implementation has been set.

_____ **United States Government Accountability Office**

Contents

Figures

Abbreviations

ABV	Assault Breacher Vehicle
AMC	Army Materiel Command
AWCF	Army Working Capital Fund
DOD	Department of Defense
HMMWV	High Mobility Multi-purpose Wheeled Vehicle
LCMC	Life Cycle Management Command
LMP	Logistics Modernization Program
OUSD	Office of the Under Secretary of Defense
RCV	Route Clearance Vehicle

GAO

U.S. GOVERNMENT ACCOUNTABILITY OFFICE

441 G St. N.W.
Washington, DC 20548

June 27, 2013

The Honorable Jeanne Shaheen
Chairman
The Honorable Kelly Ayotte
Ranking Member
Subcommittee on Readiness and Management Support
Committee on Armed Services
United States Senate

The Honorable Claire McCaskill
United States Senate

The Army operates 13 Industrial Operations activities that provide depot maintenance and ordnance services.[1] The depot maintenance services include the repair and overhaul of a wide range of vehicles and other military assets, including helicopters, such as the Apache and Black Hawk; combat vehicles, such as the Abrams tank and High Mobility Multi-purpose Wheeled Vehicles (HMMWV); and air defense systems, such as the Patriot missile. The ordnance services include manufacturing, renovating, and demilitarizing an array of defense-related munitions and components, such as howitzers, large-caliber ammunition, rockets, bombs, missiles, and incendiary devices. Many of these military assets and munitions were used to support the Army's efforts in Iraq and Afghanistan.

When Army Industrial Operations work has been ordered and funded (obligated) by customers (such as the Army) but has not been completed at the end of a fiscal year, it is referred to as carryover. The congressional defense committees have recognized that some carryover is appropriate to facilitate a smooth flow of work during the transition from one fiscal

---

[1]The 13 Industrial Operations' activities are the Anniston Army Depot, Anniston, Alabama; the Blue Grass Army Depot, Richmond, Kentucky; the Corpus Christi Army Depot, Corpus Christi, Texas; the Crane Army Ammunition Activity, Crane, Indiana; the Letterkenny Army Depot, Chambersburg, Pennsylvania; the McAlester Army Ammunition Plant, McAlester, Oklahoma; the Pine Bluff Arsenal, Pine Bluff, Arkansas; the Red River Army Depot, Texarkana, Texas; the Rock Island Arsenal-Joint Manufacturing and Technology Center, Rock Island, Illinois; the Sierra Army Depot, Herlong, California; the Tobyhanna Army Depot, Tobyhanna, Pennsylvania; the Tooele Army Depot, Tooele, Utah; and the Watervliet Arsenal, Watervliet, New York.

year to the next. However, past congressional defense committee reports have raised concerns that the level of carryover in military service working capital funds may be more than is needed. Further, excessive amounts of carryover may result in future requests being subject to reductions by the Department of Defense (DOD) and the congressional defense committees during the budget review process.

You asked us to review issues related to the Army Industrial Operations' carryover. Our objectives were to determine whether, and to what extent, Army Industrial Operations' (1) actual carryover exceeded the allowable amount of carryover from fiscal years 2006 through 2012; (2) budget information on carryover from fiscal years 2006 through 2012 approximated actual information, and if not, whether the Army took actions to align the two; and (3) carryover increased during fiscal years 2011 and 2012 and causes for the carryover for those 2 fiscal years.

To address the first and second objectives, we obtained and analyzed Army Industrial Operations reports that contained information on budgeted and actual carryover and the allowable amount of carryover for fiscal years 2006 through 2012. We analyzed carryover beginning with fiscal year 2006 because the Army's fiscal year 2006 budget reported a consolidation of the Army Working Capital Fund's (AWCF) depot maintenance and ordnance activity groups into a consolidated Industrial Operations activity group, making a comparison to prior fiscal years difficult. We met with responsible officials from the Army to obtain their views on the causes for variances between actual carryover and (1) the allowable amount and (2) budgeted carryover. We also met with these officials to discuss actions the Army has taken and is taking to reduce the amount of carryover. Further, we identified and analyzed any adjustments made by the Army that increased the allowable carryover amounts or reduced the amount of carryover. We reviewed DOD's guidance for exceptions to the carryover policy and discussed any exceptions with the Office of the Under Secretary of Defense (OUSD) (Comptroller) and Army headquarters officials to obtain explanations for the exceptions.

To address the third objective, we met with responsible Army officials to identify contributing factors that caused the carryover. Further, to corroborate the information provided by these officials, we selected eight weapon system workloads with high dollar amounts of fiscal year 2011 carryover from four Army depots. The carryover associated with these workloads represented about 35 percent of Industrial Operations' carryover for fiscal year 2011 and was one of the top five workloads with carryover at each of the four depots. We obtained and analyzed orders and amendments associated with these workloads and discussed the information in these documents with the depots to determine the causes for the carryover. Additionally, we discussed and obtained documentation on the actions the Army is taking to better manage and reduce carryover. A more detailed discussion of our scope and methodology is contained in appendix I.

We obtained the financial and logistical data in this report from official budget documents and the Army's logistical system. To assess the reliability of the data, we analyzed carryover and related data, interviewed Army officials knowledgeable about the carryover data, and reviewed customer orders to determine whether they were adequately supported by documentation. On the basis of procedures performed, we have concluded that these data were sufficiently reliable for the purposes of this report. We conducted this performance audit from May 2012 to June 2013 in accordance with generally accepted government auditing standards. Those standards require that we plan and perform the audit to obtain sufficient, appropriate evidence to provide a reasonable basis for our findings and conclusions based on our audit objectives. We believe that the evidence obtained provides a reasonable basis for our findings and conclusions based on our audit objectives. We requested comments on a draft of this report from the Secretary of Defense or his designee. Written comments from the Office of the Under Secretary of Defense (Comptroller) are reprinted in appendix II.

Background

Army Industrial Operations provides services for a variety of customers, including the Army, the Navy, the Air Force, non-DOD agencies, and foreign countries. The majority of the work is for the Army. Industrial Operations relies on sales revenue from customers to finance its continuing operations. Operating under the working capital fund concept, Industrial Operations is intended to (1) generate sufficient resources to cover the full costs of its operations and (2) operate on a break-even basis over time—that is, neither make a gain nor incur a loss. Customers, such as the Army, use appropriated funds (including operation and maintenance or procurement appropriations) to finance orders placed with Industrial Operations. Industrial Operations provides the Army an in-house industrial capability to (1) conduct depot-level maintenance, repair, and upgrade; (2) produce munitions and large-caliber weapons; and (3) store, maintain, and demilitarize material for DOD. Industrial Operations comprises 13 government-owned and operated installation activities, each with unique core competencies. These include five maintenance depots (Anniston, Alabama; Corpus Christi, Texas;

Letterkenny, Pennsylvania; Red River, Texas; and Tobyhanna, Pennsylvania), three arsenals (Pine Bluff, Arkansas; Rock Island, Illinois; and Watervliet, New York), two munitions production facilities (Crane, Indiana, and McAlester, Oklahoma), and three storage sites (Blue Grass, Kentucky; Sierra, California; and Tooele, Utah). The preponderance of the workload performed by Industrial Operations relates to depot-level maintenance.

Army Materiel Command (AMC) serves as the management command for Industrial Operations. Industrial Operations activities report under the direct command and control of the Army's Life Cycle Management Commands (LCMC), each aligned in accordance with the nature of its mission. For example, the work performed at Anniston and Red River is aligned with the Army's Tank, Automotive and Armaments Command LCMC mission of developing, acquiring, fielding, and sustaining ground systems, such as the HMMWV and Abrams tank, whereas the work performed at Letterkenny and Corpus Christi is aligned with the Army's Aviation and Missile Command LCMC mission of developing, acquiring, fielding, and sustaining aviation, missile, and unmanned vehicle systems, such as the Patriot missile and Black Hawk helicopter.

Carryover and Its Use

Carryover consists of both the unfinished portion of Army Industrial Operations work started but not completed and work that was accepted but has not yet begun. Some carryover is appropriate at the end of the fiscal year in order for working capital funds such as Industrial Operations to operate efficiently and effectively. For example, if customers do not receive new appropriations at the beginning of the fiscal year, carryover is necessary to ensure that Industrial Operations' activities (1) have enough work to continue operations in the new fiscal year and (2) retain the appropriate number of personnel with sufficient skill sets to perform depot maintenance work. Too little carryover could result in some personnel not having work to perform at the beginning of the fiscal year. On the other hand, too much carryover could result in an activity group receiving funds from customers in one fiscal year but not performing the work until well into the next fiscal year. By limiting the amount of carryover, DOD can use its resources in the most efficient and effective manner and minimize the backlog of work and "banking" of related funding for subsequent years.

DOD's Carryover Policy

DOD's Financial Management Regulation 7000.14-R, volume 2B, chapter 9, provides that the allowable amount of carryover each year is to be based on the amount of new orders received that year and the outlay rate of the customers' appropriations financing the work.[2] The DOD carryover policy further provides that the work on the current fiscal year's orders is expected to be completed by the end of the following fiscal year. DOD's Financial Management Regulation also provides that (1) nonfederal orders, non-DOD orders, foreign military sales, work related to base realignment and closure, and work-in-progress are to be excluded from the carryover calculation and (2) the reported actual carryover, net of exclusions (adjusted carryover), is then compared to the amount of allowable carryover using the above-described outlay rate method to determine whether the actual carryover amount is over or under the allowable carryover amount.[3] To the extent that adjusted carryover exceeded the allowable carryover, DOD and the congressional defense committees may reduce future budgets. According to DOD Financial Management Regulation, this carryover policy allows for an analytical-based approach that holds working capital fund activities to the same outlay standard as the general fund and allows for meaningful budget execution analysis. Requests for exceptions to the carryover policy (i.e., waivers) must be submitted to the Director for Revolving Funds, OUSD (Comptroller) separate from the budget documents. OUSD (Comptroller) officials informed us that they review requests for exceptions to the carryover policy on a case-by-case basis. Depending on the request, they may ask for additional information to evaluate the request.

Implementation of the Logistics Modernization Program

The Army implemented the Logistics Modernization Program (LMP) at two Army Industrial Operations activities in fiscal year 2009 and 10 Army Industrial Operations activities in fiscal year 2011.[4] According to the Army's budget, LMP provides the Army a modernized logistics and finance system that delivers a fully integrated suite of software and business processes, providing streamlined data on maintenance, repair and overhaul, finance, acquisition, spare parts, and materiel. LMP changed the point in time when Industrial Operations activities recognized

---

[2]The outlay rate for appropriations is contained in the DOD Financial Summary Tables, which are published each year. The outlay rate figures may vary from year to year.

[3]See DOD Financial Management Regulation 7000.14-R, *Defense Working Capital Fund Activity Group Analysis*, vol. 2B, ch. 9, p. 9-43 (June 2010), for orders excluded from the carryover calculation.

[4]One Industrial Operations activity implemented LMP in fiscal year 2003.

GAO-13-499 Army Industrial Operations

revenue. The point in time when revenue is recognized is important because when an Industrial Operations activity performs work it earns revenue and the carryover is reduced. Prior to the implementation of LMP, the Army activities recognized revenue on parts and material when the activities received the items and assigned them to orders. This procedure led, in some cases, to Industrial Operations activities buying material or spare parts and recognizing revenue and reducing carryover before the parts and material were actually used in repairing weapon systems. Under LMP, revenue is recognized when the material and parts are brought to the assembly area for installation on the weapon systems—much later in the repair process for weapon systems that have long repair cycle times.

Adjusted Carryover Was under the Allowable Amount for 5 of the Last 7 Fiscal Years

From fiscal years 2006 through 2012, the Army reported that Industrial Operations' actual carryover, adjusted for waivers/exclusions (adjusted carryover), was under the allowable amounts in 5 of the 7 fiscal years.[5] From fiscal years 2006 through 2012, Industrial Operations' total actual carryover increased from $2.3 billion to $5 billion, reaching a high of $5.8 billion—12.7 months of work—at the end of fiscal year 2011.[6] Table 1 shows the Army Industrial Operations actual adjusted carryover, allowable carryover, and the amount over (or under) the allowable carryover for fiscal years 2006 through 2012.

---

[5]Actual carryover adjusted for waivers/exclusions will be referred to as adjusted carryover in this report. The adjusted carryover amount is used when comparing it to the allowable amount. Also, waivers/exclusions will be referred to as waivers in this report.

[6]The number of months of work is a calculation to show the average time required to work off the year-end carryover amount. It is calculated by dividing total revenue earned during the year by 12 months to determine the average revenue earned by month. The total carryover at year-end is then divided by the average revenue earned by month to determine the number of months of carryover. The calculated amount represents the total number of months to perform the work, which includes labor, material, and overhead costs.

Table 1: Comparison of Army Industrial Operations' Actual Adjusted Carryover and Allowable Carryover (Fiscal Years 2006 through 2012)

Dollars in millions

Fiscal year	Actual adjusted carryover	Allowable carryover	Actual over (under) allowable amount
2006	$2,141	$2,115	$26
2007	3,030	2,752	277
2008	2,862	3,654	(792)
2009	3,146	3,327	(181)
2010	3,452	4,076	(624)
2011	4,321	4,684	(363)
2012	4,573	4,768	(194)

Source: GAO analysis of Army Industrial Operations data.

Note: Actual over (under) allowable dollar amounts for fiscal years 2007 and 2012 do not add because of rounding.

While actual adjusted carryover was under the allowable amount in the most recent 5-year period, total carryover increased by about 117 percent from fiscal years 2006 through 2012. The total carryover increased from about 6 months of work in fiscal year 2006 to 9.5 months in fiscal year 2012, and reached its highest point in fiscal year 2011 at 12.7 months of work. Figure 1 depicts Army Industrial Operations' actual new orders, revenue, and total carryover and shows the total amount of work that carried over without the adjustments.

Figure 1: Army Industrial Operations' New Orders, Revenue, and Total Carryover (Fiscal Years 2006 through 2012)

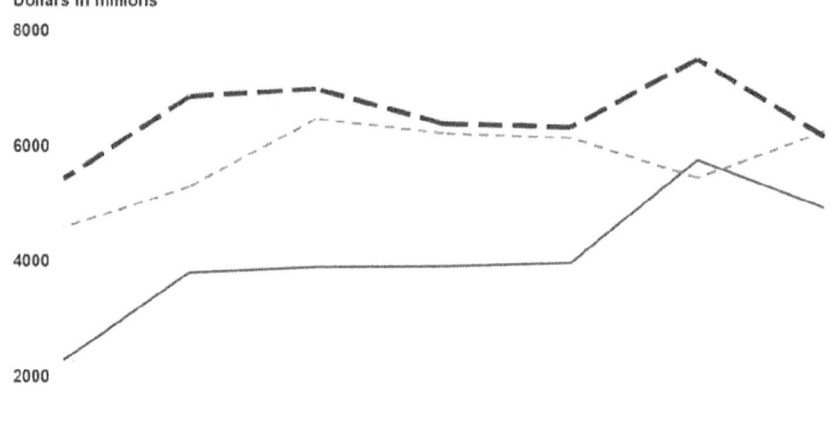

	2006	2007	2008	2009	2010	2011	2012
New orders (Actual)	$5,425	$6,850	$6,991	$6,393	$6,340	$7,529	$6,189
Revenue (Actual)	$4,592	$5,286	$6,471	$6,229	$6,157	$5,469	$6,283
Carryover (Actual)	$2,281	$3,800	$3,900	$3,919	$3,984	$5,776	$4,960
Months of carryover (Actual)	6.0	8.6	7.2	7.6	7.8	12.7	9.5

Source: GAO analysis of Army Industrial Operations budgets.

Note: The carryover amounts are the total carryover amounts and are not adjusted for waivers.

In September 2011, the Army requested and OUSD (Comptroller) approved three waivers that had not been requested by the Army in prior years. The Army and OUSD (Comptroller) followed the procedures for requesting and approving waivers contained in the DOD Financial Management Regulation. The Army provided OUSD (Comptroller) a memo requesting the waivers and provided justifications for the waivers. OUSD (Comptroller) approved the Army's waiver request. The effect of these waivers was that the Army reported that its Industrial Operations' adjusted carryover was under the allowable amount by $363 million at the end of fiscal year 2011. Absent these waivers, Industrial Operations would have been over the allowable amount by about $1 billion for fiscal year 2011. The Army requested and OUSD (Comptroller) approved two similar waivers in fiscal year 2012, and the Army reported that Industrial

Operations was under the allowable amount by $194 million for fiscal year 2012. Without the new waivers that it received in fiscal year 2012, Industrial Operations would have been over the allowable amount by $1.2 billion for fiscal year 2012.

According to the Army's waiver request and OUSD (Comptroller) approval memorandums, the new waivers consisted of (1) excluding the HMMWV fiscal year 2011 orders and related carryover from the carryover calculation for fiscal year 2011 because Industrial Operations did not receive the HMMWV orders until late in the fiscal year, precluding the Army from executing any significant amount of work during fiscal year 2011; (2) using outlay rates published in the Inflation Guidance instead of the outlay rates published in the DOD Financial Summary Tables for operation and maintenance-funded orders for calculating the allowable carryover for fiscal years 2011 and 2012 because the outlay rates in the Inflation Guidance more accurately reflect the nature of the carryover work; and (3) allowing the Army to use second year outlay rates for all procurement-funded orders for calculating the allowable carryover for fiscal years 2011 and 2012 because the scope and complexity of procurement-funded orders require longer lead time to perform the work.

We discussed the new waivers with Army headquarters officials and the circumstances that led to the requests for the new waivers. According to these officials, fiscal year 2011 was an abnormal year. Specifically, in fiscal year 2011, Industrial Operations received more orders than it had ever received in a single year—$7.5 billion in new orders. Further, Industrial Operations received $839 million in orders for the HMMWV work late in the fiscal year—June 2011—allowing little time to perform work on these orders by the end of the fiscal year. The Army also implemented LMP at 10 Industrial Operations activities in fiscal year 2011, which changed the business rules for recognizing revenue and therefore resulted in carryover being higher than it would have been under the prior system. However, Army officials could not tell us the dollar impact that the implementation of LMP had on carryover. Because new orders increased and revenue decreased due to the change in business rules, carryover grew to $5.8 billion, or 12.7 months of work, at the end of fiscal year 2011. It was for these reasons that the Army requested the new waivers.

Army officials stated that fiscal year 2012 was also an abnormal year because Industrial Operations needed to work off the $5.8 billion carryover balance that existed at the end of fiscal year 2011. To reduce the carryover, Industrial Operations worked multiple shifts and overtime on some production lines during fiscal year 2012. As a result, the amount of carryover decreased to just under $5 billion at the end of fiscal year 2012—9.5 months of work. Army officials also informed us that they anticipate carryover further decreasing at the end of fiscal year 2013. According to Industrial Operations' fiscal year 2014 budget, the amount of carryover at the end of fiscal year 2013 is expected to be under $4 billion.

Budgeted Information on Carryover Underestimated Actual Carryover Information, but the Army Began Taking Action to Align These in Fiscal Year 2012

The Army's budget estimates for its Industrial Operations carryover were consistently less than the actual carryover amounts each year from fiscal years 2006 through 2012. For the 7-year period, the Industrial Operations actual carryover exceeded budgeted carryover by at least $1.1 billion each year. This was primarily because (1) the Army underestimated its Industrial Operations new orders received from customers for each of the 7 years and (2) for fiscal year 2011, Industrial Operations performed over $1 billion less work than budgeted. Reliable budget information on carryover is critical because decision makers use this information when reviewing Industrial Operations budgets. Table 2 compares the dollar amounts of the Army's budgeted and actual Industrial Operations carryover and the difference between these amounts for fiscal years 2006 through 2012.

Table 2: Comparison of Budgeted and Actual Army Industrial Operations' Carryover (Fiscal Years 2006 through 2012)

Dollars in millions

Fiscal year	Budgeted carryover	Actual carryover	Difference
2006	$1,149	$2,281	($1,132)
2007	1,282	3,800	(2,519)
2008	2,370	3,900	(1,530)
2009	2,811	3,919	(1,109)
2010	2,602	3,984	(1,382)
2011	3,295	5,776	(2,481)
2012	2,968	4,960	(1,992)

Source: GAO analysis of Army's Industrial Operations budgets.

Note: Dollar amounts do not always add because of rounding.

Army's Budget Significantly Underestimated New Orders

One factor we found that contributed to actual carryover exceeding budgeted carryover by over $1 billion annually over the 7-year period was that the Army significantly underestimated the amount of new orders to be received from its Industrial Operations customers. As shown in table 3, from fiscal years 2006 through 2012, Army Industrial Operations budgeted to receive about $35.6 billion in new orders, but Industrial Operations reports showed that it actually received about $45.7 billion in new orders. As a result, Industrial Operations underestimated new orders received from customers by about $10.1 billion over the 7-year period.

Table 3: Army Industrial Operations' Budgeted New Orders Compared to Actual New Orders (Fiscal Years 2006 through 2012)

Dollars in millions

Fiscal year	Budgeted new orders	Actual new orders	Dollar variance	Percentage variance
2006	$3,188	$5,425	$2,237	70
2007	4,562	6,850	2,288	50
2008	6,300	6,991	691	11
2009	5,016	6,393	1,377	27
2010	5,715	6,340	625	11
2011	6,163	7,529	1,366	22
2012	4,672	6,189	1,517	32
Total	$35,616	$45,718	$10,102	28

Source: GAO analysis of Army Industrial Operations budgets.

Note: Dollar amounts do not always add because of rounding.

We analyzed the appropriations funding new orders to determine which appropriation had the largest variance. The Army's total budgeted new order amounts for the 7-year period were within 15 percent of the total actual new order amounts for the operation and maintenance and other appropriations categories. The largest differences for these two appropriation categories occurred in fiscal years 2006 and 2007, when Industrial Operations budget assumptions in support of the Global War on

Terrorism underestimated the amount of orders actually received.[7] However, over the same period, our analysis of budgeted and actual orders showed that actual new orders funded by the procurement appropriation category exceeded budgeted new orders by about $5.8 billion, or 118 percent. Actual amounts funded by the procurement appropriation category exceeded budgeted amounts by over 50 percent in all but one year, with actual amounts exceeding budgeted amounts by more than 100 percent in 4 of the 7 years. Table 4 shows Army Industrial Operations' budgeted new orders compared to actual new orders by appropriation category funding the orders for fiscal years 2006 through 2012.

Table 4: Army Industrial Operations' Budgeted New Orders Compared to Actual New Orders by Appropriation Category Funding the Orders (Fiscal Years 2006 through 2012)

Dollars in million

Fiscal year	Operation and Maintenance			Procurement			Other appropriations		
	Budget	Actual	Percentage variance	Budget	Actual	Percentage variance	Budget	Actual	Percentage variance
2006	$1,599	$2,502	57	$284	$1,182	316	$1,305	$1,741	33
2007	2,264	3,474	53	767	1,462	91	1,532	1,914	25
2008	3,828	3,056	(20)	642	1,726	169	1,831	2,209	21
2009	2,671	2,909	9	573	1,543	169	1,771	1,942	10
2010	2,866	3,130	9	1,034	1,238	20	1,815	1,972	9
2011	2,783	3,299	19	1,283	2,295	79	2,097	1,936	(8)
2012	2,723	3,076	13	352	1,338	280	1,596	1,774	11
Total	**$18,734**	**$21,446**	**14**	**$4,936**	**$10,784**	**118**	**$11,946**	**$13,487**	**13**

Source: GAO analysis of Army Industrial Operations budgets.

Note: Dollar amounts do not always add because of rounding.

Army headquarters and AMC officials stated that they recognized that Army Industrial Operations had difficulty in accurately budgeting for new orders, particularly for procurement-funded orders and carryover. In

---

[7]Our analysis of the AWCF budget guidance for fiscal year 2006 showed that the Army assumed that the fiscal year 2006 new orders amount would approximate 50 percent of the fiscal year 2005 operation and maintenance supplemental budget. For fiscal year 2007, the Army assumed that the fiscal year 2007 orders would be approximately 25 percent less than the fiscal year 2006 program. These assumptions resulted in the budgeted orders for fiscal years 2006 and 2007 being lower than the actual reported orders for these 2 fiscal years.

GAO-13-499 Army Industrial Operations

discussing this matter with Army headquarters officials, the officials stated that Industrial Operations develops its budgets based on information from customers. However, Industrial Operations underestimated the amount of new orders because (1) the customers did not always notify Industrial Operations of their plans to provide some orders, (2) the customers did not always commit to providing some orders, and (3) customer requirements subsequently changed from the time they prepared their budgets to the time the orders were placed with Industrial Operations. The Army officials we spoke with stated that improved communications between Industrial Operations and customers is needed to help better ensure that budgeted orders approximate actual orders. Specifically, they stated that customers and Industrial Operations need to work together so that Industrial Operations receives reliable new order information to be included in its budgets.

To improve the management of carryover, the Army formed a working group in April 2012. Among other things, the working group identified that improved planning and communication was needed on budgeting for orders. The working group identified a number of actions that have the potential for remedying the budgeting and actual carryover and order variances, including the following:

- Holding a series of monthly or quarterly meetings to better manage carryover, including issues related to orders received from customers. For example, beginning in July 2012, AMC and the LCMCs and their individual activities began to hold quarterly meetings that provide information on the status of Industrial Operations' carryover, orders, and revenue. Production issues for specific workloads and strategies to reduce carryover are discussed at these meetings. Strategies aimed at increasing revenue and reducing carryover include working a second shift at the activities or actions to obtain long lead time parts.

- Establishing a policy on acceptance of unscheduled new orders.

- Requiring the program managers (customers) to clearly identify planned depot work in their procurement budgets so Industrial Operations can better determine the dollar amount of budgeted orders funded with procurement appropriations.

In addition, AMC has taken or plans to take the following actions intended to improve the management and budgeting of Industrial Operations' carryover and orders.

- AMC reviewed orders received by Industrial Operations from customers in the fourth quarter of fiscal year 2012 and disapproved some orders that were unplanned and not included in the Industrial Operations fiscal year 2012 budget because the orders would increase fiscal year 2012 carryover. Specifically, AMC disapproved $97 million of orders received from Industrial Operations' customers.

- During fiscal year 2013, the Army plans to better align the customers' budgets with the Industrial Operations budgets. AMC identified three points during the budget and requirements process at which budget information on orders can be updated with the most current workload data. At these points, AMC, the LCMCs, and the Industrial Operations activities will meet with their customers, including the Office of the Assistant Secretary of the Army (Acquisition, Logistics and Technology), the Army National Guard, and the Army Reserve, and review the customers' requirements and update the Industrial Operations budgets for any orders to be received.

If fully and effectively implemented, these actions should help address the order and carryover budgeting issues. However, the Army has not yet developed a timetable for implementing the actions identified by the working group.

Army Earned Less Revenue Than Budgeted in Fiscal Year 2011

Our analysis of Army Industrial Operations budget documents showed that Industrial Operations earned less revenue than budgeted in fiscal year 2011, contributing to actual carryover exceeding the budgeted amount by $2.5 billion for fiscal year 2011. Even though the total budgeted and actual revenue was nearly equal from fiscal years 2006 through 2012, Industrial Operations' budget data also showed that Industrial Operations' actual revenue for fiscal year 2011 fell below budgeted revenue by about $1 billion and below the previous year's results by $688 million. Table 5 shows a comparison between budgeted and actual revenue for fiscal years 2006 through 2012.

Table 5: Army Industrial Operations' Budgeted Revenue Compared to Actual Revenue (Fiscal Years 2006 through 2012)

Dollars in millions

Fiscal year	Budgeted revenue	Actual revenue	Dollar variance	Percentage variance
2006	$3,992	$4,592	$600	15
2007	4,784	5,286	502	10
2008	6,673	6,471	(202)	(3)
2009	5,930	6,229	299	5
2010	6,309	6,157	(152)	(2)
2011	6,505	5,469	(1,035)	(16)
2012	5,134	6,283	1,149	22
Total	**$39,325**	**$40,486**	**$1,161**	**3**

Source: GAO analysis of Army Industrial Operations budgets.

Note: Dollar amounts do not always add because of rounding.

Army officials stated that the implementation of LMP at the Industrial Operations activities in fiscal years 2009 and 2011 contributed to the fiscal year 2011 actual revenue falling below the prior year and budgeted amounts. First, in the first quarter of fiscal year 2011, LMP was implemented at 10 of the 13 Industrial Operations activities. At the deployment activities, revenue was lower in fiscal year 2011 because of production delays caused by the workforce being unfamiliar with the revised LMP requirements. Second, when the fiscal year 2011 Industrial Operations budget was developed in the summer of 2009, 2 of the 13 Industrial Operations activities had just deployed LMP and 10 of the 13 had not yet deployed LMP. The LCMCs and the activities did not fully understand the impact LMP would have on revenue recognition at the time of their budget submissions, resulting in actual revenue being less than budgeted.

Carryover Increased at the End of Fiscal Years 2011 and 2012 and Was Caused by Several Factors

Much of the growth in Army Industrial Operations' carryover occurred in the past 2 fiscal years. During this period, carryover grew from $2.3 billion at the end of fiscal year 2006 to a high of $5.8 billion at the end of fiscal year 2011. Carryover grew in fiscal year 2011 because Industrial Operations received more orders ($7.5 billion) than work it performed ($5.5 billion). At the end of fiscal year 2012, carryover totaled about $5 billion.

We analyzed eight workloads that accounted for $2 billion of the $5.8 billion in carryover at the end of fiscal year 2011. The carryover associated with these workloads represented about 35 percent of Industrial Operations' carryover for fiscal year 2011. In analyzing these workloads, we found three primary causes for the carryover: (1) the scope of work was not well defined, (2) parts needed to perform the work were not available, and (3) revenue recognition business rules were changed as part of the implementation of LMP. As an additional cause, the Industrial Operations activities accepted some orders in the third and fourth quarters of fiscal year 2011, which provided them little time to resolve any scope of work or parts issues in fiscal year 2011. Table 6 summarizes the results of our analysis of the key causes of carryover related to the eight workloads we analyzed.

Table 6: Analysis of Key Causes for Carryover for Eight Army Industrial Operations Workloads

| Workloads | Key causes for carryover | | |
	Scope of work not well defined	Parts not available	Change in revenue recognition rules
Ammunition Rack		✓	
Assault Breacher Vehicle		✓	
Aviation Ground Power Unit	✓	✓	
Black Hawk			✓
Force Provider		✓	✓
High Mobility Multi-purpose Wheeled Vehicle		✓	
Patriot Radar		✓	
Route Clearance Vehicle	✓	✓	

Source: GAO analysis of eight Army Industrial Operations workloads.

Scope of Work Not Well Defined

In order for the Army Industrial Operations activities to perform work in a timely manner and minimize carryover, the activities should have a well-defined scope of work, including approved technical data and documented processes. Industrial Operations officials informed us that the lack of a well-defined scope of work was one of the causes of carryover. Our analysis of eight Industrial Operations workloads corroborated the information provided by Industrial Operations officials and found that work on two workloads was delayed and carryover increased because the scope of work was not well defined.

For example, in July 2010, Letterkenny accepted its first order to convert 3 Mine Resistant Ambush Protected vehicles to a different operational purpose. The converted vehicle is referred to as a Route Clearance Vehicle (RCV).[8] Under the accepted work order, Letterkenny was expected to design and engineer 3 prototype vehicles, establish a technical data package to convert the vehicles, and develop a statement of work and a bill of materials. The 3 vehicles were expected to be completed by December 2010—about 6 months later. However, the depot experienced problems designing the modified vehicle, reaching agreement with its customer on the new design, and performing tests on the first vehicle. The final technical data package to convert the additional vehicles and the development of the statement of work and the bill of materials were delayed until the new design was agreed upon and the first vehicle was tested. As the depot continued to work with its customer on the design of the 3 pilot vehicles, in July 2011, Letterkenny accepted its second order under this program for the production of 10 vehicles. One month later, the depot accepted a third order for over 300 production vehicles for $211 million. Because of the delays in completing the 3 prototype vehicles that were to identify the specifications of the work to be performed, the depot carried over about $211 million in work orders into fiscal year 2012.

Moreover, the depot had a total of three pilot vehicles and 292 production vehicles on order at the end of fiscal year 2012.[9] One pilot vehicle ordered was almost complete as of September 30, 2012. The depot carried over about $209 million in work orders into fiscal year 2013. A photo of a Mine Resistant Ambush Protected vehicle that is being converted to an RCV is shown in figure 2.

---

[8]The RCV is a vehicle for route clearance and explosive ordnance disposal.

[9]The production vehicle quantities decreased from fiscal years 2011 through 2012 because the unit funded cost per vehicle increased.

Figure 2: Mine Resistant Ambush Protected Vehicle Being Converted to a Route Clearance Vehicle

Source: Army Materiel Command.

Parts Not Readily Available to Perform Repair Work

Without the right mix and sufficient quantity of spare parts, the Army Industrial Operations activities are impaired in their ability to complete their funded workloads in a timely and efficient manner. Industrial Operations officials informed us that parts shortages was one of the causes of carryover. Our analysis of Industrial Operations data corroborated these officials' views and found that parts shortages at the activities contributed to carryover for seven of the eight workloads we reviewed. Parts were not available for work to proceed in a timely manner because (1) the depots accepted orders funded with procurement appropriations in fiscal year 2011 but contracts to purchase parts needed to perform the work were not awarded until fiscal years 2012 or 2013 and (2) the HMMWV work outpaced the ability of the supply chain to provide the parts. The delay in receipt of parts extended the time needed for the activities to complete work on the orders which, in turn, increased the amount of work that carried over into the following fiscal year or fiscal years. For example, as summarized in figure 3 and discussed in more detail below, parts shortages impaired Industrial Operations' depots at Red River and Letterkenny from completing their HMMWV work orders.

GAO-13-499 Army Industrial Operations

Figure 3: Overview of Impact of Parts Shortages on Completing HMMWV Work Orders at Red River and Letterkenny

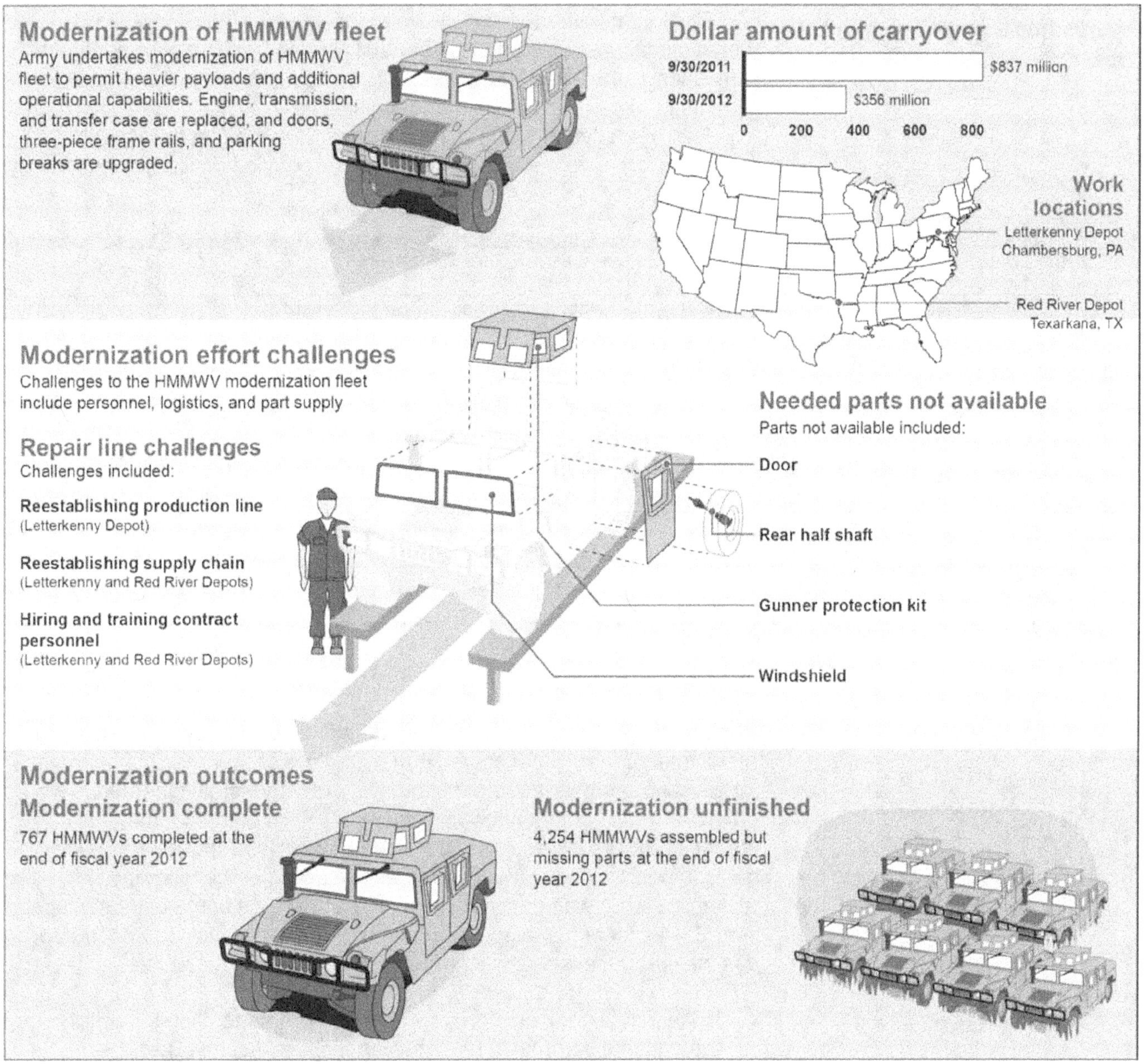

Modernization of HMMWV fleet

Army undertakes modernization of HMMWV fleet to permit heavier payloads and additional operational capabilities. Engine, transmission, and transfer case are replaced, and doors, three-piece frame rails, and parking breaks are upgraded.

Dollar amount of carryover

9/30/2011 — $837 million
9/30/2012 — $356 million

0   200   400   600   800

Work locations

Letterkenny Depot
Chambersburg, PA

Red River Depot
Texarkana, TX

Modernization effort challenges

Challenges to the HMMWV modernization fleet include personnel, logistics, and part supply

Repair line challenges

Challenges included:

Reestablishing production line
(Letterkenny Depot)

Reestablishing supply chain
(Letterkenny and Red River Depots)

Hiring and training contract personnel
(Letterkenny and Red River Depots)

Needed parts not available

Parts not available included:

— Door

— Rear half shaft

— Gunner protection kit

— Windshield

Modernization outcomes

Modernization complete

767 HMMWVs completed at the end of fiscal year 2012

Modernization unfinished

4,254 HMMWVs assembled but missing parts at the end of fiscal year 2012

Source: GAO analysis of Letterkenny and Red River data.

Contracts to Purchase Parts Were Awarded 1 or 2 Fiscal Years after Depots Accepted Orders

Our analysis of Army order and contract data associated with five workloads found that contracts for critical parts were not awarded until 1 or 2 fiscal years after the orders were accepted by the depots. This resulted in almost all the fiscal year 2011 funds carrying over on these workloads at the end of fiscal year 2011 and funds on these orders continuing to carry over at the end of fiscal year 2012. Table 7 shows the workload, description of the parts ordered, date the first fiscal year 2011 order was accepted, contract award date for buying critical parts, and key contract terms.

Table 7: Key Dates and Contract Terms for Five Army Industrial Operations Workloads

Workload	Description of parts ordered	Order acceptance date[a]	Contract award date	Key contract terms
Ammunition Rack	Ammunition rack upgrade kits	April 2011	September 2012	Six months to first delivery
Assault Breacher Vehicle	Conversion assembly kits	August 2011	December 2011	Production of three per month
Aviation Ground Power Unit	Engines	June 2011	June 2012	Production of eight per month
Force Provider	Storage and transportation containers	January 2011	August 2012	Delivery begins within 30 days
Route Clearance Vehicle	Conversion parts	July 2011	November 2012	First delivery February 2013

Source: GAO analysis of Army order and contract data.

[a]Date the first fiscal year 2011 order was accepted by the depot. Some workloads had multiple orders in fiscal year 2011.

Work on the five fiscal year 2011 workloads shown above was delayed to fiscal year 2012 or 2013 because of the timing of the award of contracts for critical parts needed to complete the Army Industrial Operations work orders. For four of the five workloads, the award of the contracts to purchase parts occurred 1 or more years after the depot received the order to perform the work. Further, as illustrated in the following examples, work was delayed in fiscal year 2012 on some of these fiscal year 2011 orders because of the terms of the contracts—the contractor can only produce a certain number per month.

- In August 2011, Anniston accepted five orders totaling $44 million for the conversion of 20 M1A1 Abrams tanks to Assault Breacher Vehicles (ABV). In order to perform the work, Anniston had to remove the old turrets, fabricate new turrets, and convert the tank hulls to address the vehicles' new function—to breach mine fields and barrier obstacles. Anniston officials told us that they could not begin work on the orders until they received material (government-furnished equipment) that was being procured by the program manager. However, the contract to procure the government-furnished equipment was not awarded until December 2011—fiscal year 2012— and the contractor could only produce three kits per month. Anniston began work on the ABV orders in May 2012 so that the work fell in line with the delivery of the government-furnished equipment. As a result, the first vehicle on the order was not completed until October 2012—fiscal year 2013—and the production of the vehicles at Anniston was limited to three per month to match the supplier's ability to manufacture the needed kits. The depot carried over the entire amount into fiscal year 2012 and $25 million into fiscal year 2013.

During fiscal year 2012, Anniston accepted five more ABV Army orders totaling $48.3 million to produce 22 ABVs and almost all the work—$46.3 million—carried over into fiscal year 2013. Similar to the orders accepted in fiscal year 2011, Anniston had to maintain a low monthly production quantity because one of the contractors could only deliver three material kits per month. A photo of an ABV is shown in figure 4.

Figure 4: Assault Breacher Vehicle

Source: Army Materiel Command.

- Letterkenny received four orders in the second quarter of fiscal year 2011 totaling $156 million for 17 Force Provider modules.[10] Letterkenny procures equipment to fill approximately 43 of the 101 containers that make up each new build module. The 43 containers hold approximately 346 different types of new equipment comprising thousands of individual components. Letterkenny carried over almost the entire amount into fiscal year 2012—$156 million.

In fiscal year 2012, Letterkenny accepted three more orders totaling $18 million for six new Force Providers. However, a contract was not awarded to buy containers until August 2012—over a year after receiving the first fiscal year 2011 order. Letterkenny received about 700 containers from August through December 2012. In the meantime, work essentially stopped on the new build program in July and August 2012 because of the lack of sufficient containers to complete 13 of the 17 modules on the fiscal year 2011 orders and 6 modules on the fiscal year 2012 orders. Without the containers, the depot could not complete work on the fiscal years 2011 and 2012 orders and reduce carryover on the orders. The depot carried over $79 million into fiscal year 2013 associated with the fiscal year 2011 and 2012 new build orders. A photo of a Force Provider is shown in figure 5.

[10]The Force Provider is a transportable base camp system that provides housing and operational space for a variety of missions.

Figure 5: Force Provider

Source: Army Materiel Command.

Required Parts Exceeded Available Supplies, Which Impaired Depots' Ability to Perform HMMWV Work

The work that Red River and Letterkenny performed on the HMMWV in fiscal years 2011 and 2012 outpaced the ability of the supply chain to provide the parts. In June 2011, Red River and Letterkenny accepted orders to overhaul 7,971 HMMWVs.[11] At the end of fiscal year 2011, the amount of the orders was $839 million, and of that amount, $837 million carried over into fiscal year 2012. In order to perform the work on these vehicles, Letterkenny had to reestablish its production line since it was previously shut down because of the lack of HMMWV work. Further, both depots had to hire contractor personnel to staff the production line and establish a supply chain so that the depots could obtain the parts to perform the work. Both depots encountered problems with obtaining sufficient quantities of parts, such as doors, gunner protection kits, windshields, turret bearings, and half shafts, to perform the work. This parts problem was exacerbated at Red River when the depot went to a

---

[11]The customer reduced the quantity from 7,971 to 6,957 HMMWVs in October 2012.

double shift on disassembling and assembling HMMWVs in April 2012. As a result of the parts shortage, at the end of fiscal year 2012, Red River and Letterkenny completed 767 of the vehicles ordered in fiscal year 2011. In addition, the depots assembled another 4,254 vehicles but the vehicles were missing parts. The depots carried over $356 million of these orders into fiscal year 2013. A photo of a HMMWV is shown in figure 6.

Figure 6: High Mobility Multi-purpose Wheeled Vehicle

Source: Army Materiel Command.

Changed Revenue Recognition Business Rules under LMP

As discussed previously, the implementation of LMP changed the revenue recognition business rules and resulted in increased carryover in fiscal years 2011 and 2012. The point in time when revenue is recognized is important because when an Army Industrial Operations activity performs work, it earns revenue, thereby reducing carryover. As discussed earlier, the Army implemented LMP at two Industrial Operations activities in fiscal year 2009 and 10 Industrial Operations activities in fiscal year 2011. While the Army could not determine the extent of the change on Industrial Operations' carryover resulting from implementation of LMP, officials at Army headquarters, LCMCs, and the depots stated that they believed carryover increased because of the change in revenue recognition rules.

For example, Corpus Christi reported in fiscal year 2011 that it accepted orders totaling about $455 million to repair and upgrade 57 Black Hawk helicopters. The established repair process time for the UH-60L Black Hawk averaged approximately 1 year in fiscal year 2011. The change in the business rules for recognizing revenue on parts and material because of the implementation of LMP in May 2009 caused revenue on the fiscal year 2011 orders to be recognized, or earned, in fiscal year 2012. Prior to the implementation of LMP, the depot's business rules recognized revenue on parts and material on the Black Hawk when they were turned into the supply system during the disassembly process and replacement parts were requisitioned and received—usually within the first 90 days. Under LMP, revenue for parts and material is not recognized until parts and material are brought to the assembly area for installation on the aircraft. Final assembly of the aircraft occurs about 266 days after acceptance of the orders. As a result, at least in part due to the change in revenue recognition rules under LMP, at the end of fiscal year 2011, Corpus Christi documentation showed that it carried over into the next fiscal year $425 million associated with these orders—93 percent of the order amounts. A photo of a Black Hawk helicopter is shown in figure 7.

Figure 7: Black Hawk Helicopter

Source: Army Material Command.

Army Has Actions Under Way and Planned to Improve Management of Carryover

Because of the size of the carryover at the end of fiscal year 2011, the Army recognized that it needed to improve its management of carryover, and in April 2012, the Army formed a working group. The working group identified, among other things, that it was the Army Industrial Operations activities' responsibility to ensure that they have the necessary resources for performing the work. The working group identified the following six elements that the Industrial Operations activities should review when receiving orders for work to be performed:

- Skilled labor. Are there adequate labor hours available with the required skills to execute the work?

- Parts. Is there sufficient stock on hand or in the supply pipeline to complete the program schedule on time?

- Tools and equipment. Are all required special tools, fixtures, jigs, and stands on hand or being acquired?

- Process. Is there approved technical data, including a defined scope of work, documented processes, and internal process capacity, available to complete the work?

- Requirements. Is there an understanding of the total Army requirements as well as the required depot production for the workload after considering back orders, average monthly demand, potential surge requirements, and alternate source of repair?

- Funding. Is there available funding and rate of required funding to support production?

Further, the working group determined that if the Industrial Operations activities determine that they do not have the capability to perform any of the six elements, the activities should be required to send orders to their management for review and approval. Also, for any areas for which resources are not available, the activities should be required to develop a plan on how they will resolve the issue, such as obtaining parts that are not in the supply system.

To convey the working group's results, the Army plans to issue two policy memos during fiscal year 2013. According to Army officials and documentation we reviewed, one policy memo will address (1) the LCMCs' and activities' responsibilities for acceptance of orders and performing the work (regardless of the appropriation funding the orders) and (2) the six elements discussed above. The second policy memo will address orders funded with procurement appropriations. According to Army officials, this second policy memo will discuss various aspects of procurement-funded orders, including different types of work such as pilot programs, prototypes, fabrication, and data requirements. According to the Army, this action should result in a better alignment of the work to the customer delivery schedule and prevent the acceptance of workloads that are not executable in a specific fiscal year. We agree that these actions are needed for orders placed with Industrial Operations. If properly implemented, the Army's actions should help address our concerns that (1) the scope of work was not well defined and (2) parts were not available to perform the work. However, the Army has not issued the planned policy memos. The memos should contain specific timetables for implementing their planned actions and establish procedures to include steps to be followed by Industrial Operations in evaluating orders received from customers.

Conclusions

The work that Army Industrial Operations performs supports combat readiness by restoring equipment to a level of combat capability commensurate with a unit's future mission. Reliable budgeted information on Industrial Operations, including carryover information, is essential for Congress and DOD to perform their oversight responsibilities, including reviewing and making well-informed decisions on Industrial Operations budgets. The Army reported in its budgets to Congress that Industrial Operations' adjusted carryover was under the allowable amount at the end of fiscal years 2011 and 2012. However, budget estimates for carryover were consistently less than the actual amounts each year from fiscal years 2006 through 2012 primarily because of Industrial Operations underestimating new orders from customers, particularly procurement-funded orders. Budget estimates could be improved by addressing the major factors that caused variations between budgeted and actual amounts, including improved communication between customers and Industrial Operations. The Army recognized that it needed to improve the budgeting and management of carryover and formed a working group in April 2012. The working group identified a number of actions that are under way and planned to help remedy this situation. However, the Army has not yet implemented these planned actions and does not have a timetable for implementation.

Recommendations for Executive Action

We recommend that the Secretary of Defense direct the Secretary of the Army to take the following three actions to improve the budgeting and management of Army Industrial Operations' carryover:

- Issue the planned working group policy memos and establish a timetable for implementing these actions for improving the management of carryover.

- Implement the working group's planned actions to improve the budgeting for new orders to be received by Army Industrial Operations.

- Establish procedures, including required steps, to be followed by Army Industrial Operations activities in evaluating orders received from customers to ensure that the activities have resources (such as parts and materials, skilled labor, tools, equipment, technical data, and funding) to perform the work.

Agency Comments

DOD provided written comments on a draft of this report. In its comments, which are reprinted in appendix II, DOD concurred with the three recommendations and cited actions planned or under way to address them. Specifically, DOD commented that by the end of fiscal year 2013, the Army will issue policy memorandums with actions to be implemented by the beginning of the second quarter of fiscal year 2014. The memorandums will address the following: (1) the responsibilities and criteria of the Industrial Operations activities to accept new orders whether budgeted or unbudgeted and (2) new procurement-funded orders to better align the work to customer delivery schedules. Further, DOD stated that the Army's fiscal year 2014 budget guidance included direction for program managers to identify planned depot workload in procurement budgets beginning in the fiscal year 2014 President's Budget cycle and that the same direction will be included in subsequent budget cycle guidance. Finally, DOD indicated that the Army will establish procedures to implement the policy memorandum on the acceptance of new orders beginning with the second quarter of fiscal year 2014.

We are sending copies of this report to the appropriate congressional committees, the Secretary of Defense, and the Secretary of the Army. In addition, the report is available at no charge on the GAO website at http://www.gao.gov.

If you or your staff have any questions about this report, please contact me at (202) 512-9869 or khana@gao.gov. Contact points for our Offices of Congressional Relations and Public Affairs may be found on the last page of this report. Key contributors to this report are listed in appendix III.

Asif A. Khan
Director, Financial Management and Assurance

Appendix I: Scope and Methodology

To determine whether, and to what extent, Army Industrial Operations' actual carryover exceeded the allowable amount of carryover from fiscal years 2006 through 2012, we obtained and analyzed Industrial Operations reports that contained information on actual carryover and the allowable amount of carryover for fiscal years 2006 through 2012. We analyzed carryover beginning with fiscal year 2006 because the Army's fiscal year 2006 budget reported a consolidation of the Army Working Capital Fund's depot maintenance and ordnance activity groups into Industrial Operations, making a comparison to prior fiscal years difficult. We met with responsible officials from Army headquarters and Army Materiel Command (AMC) to obtain their views on the causes for variances between actual carryover and the allowable amount. Further, we identified and analyzed any adjustments made by the Army that increased the allowable carryover amounts or reduced the amount of carryover. We reviewed the Department of Defense's guidance for exceptions to the carryover policy and discussed any exceptions with Office of the Under Secretary of Defense (OUSD) (Comptroller) and Army headquarters officials to obtain explanations for the exceptions.

To determine whether, and to what extent, Army Industrial Operations' budget information on carryover from fiscal years 2006 through 2012 approximated actual information, and if not, whether the Army took actions to align the two, we obtained and analyzed Industrial Operations reports that contained information on budgeted and reported actual new orders, revenue, and actual carryover data for fiscal years 2006 through 2012. We also analyzed the new order data by the appropriations financing the orders to determine whether there were variances by appropriations for budgeted and reported actual new order amounts for the 7-year period. We met with responsible officials from Army headquarters and AMC to obtain their views on causes for variances between budgeted and reported actual new order, revenue, and carryover amounts. We also met with these officials to discuss actions the Army was taking to improve budgeting and management of carryover.

To determine whether, and to what extent, Army Industrial Operations' carryover increased during fiscal years 2011 and 2012, and causes for the carryover for those 2 fiscal years, we met with responsible officials from Army headquarters, AMC, the Office of the Assistant Secretary of the Army (Acquisition, Logistics and Technology), the Life Cycle Management Commands (LCMC), and four depots that had orders with high dollar amounts of fiscal year 2011 carryover to identify contributing factors that caused the carryover. We also performed walk-throughs of the Army's Anniston, Corpus Christi, Letterkenny, and Red River depots' operations to observe the work being performed by the depots and discussed with officials causes for workload carrying over from one fiscal year to the next. Further, to corroborate the information provided by Industrial Operations officials, we selected eight weapon system workloads with high dollar amounts of fiscal year 2011 carryover from four Army depots. The carryover associated with these workloads represented about 35 percent of Industrial Operations' total carryover at the end of fiscal year 2011 and was one of the top five workloads with carryover at each depot. We followed up on the status of carryover on these eight workloads at the end of fiscal year 2012. We obtained and analyzed orders and amendments associated with these workloads and discussed the information in these documents with the depots to determine the causes for the carryover. We discussed the carryover information on these workloads with officials in the program management offices at the Office of the Assistant Secretary of the Army (Acquisition, Logistics and Technology) to determine their roles and responsibilities in providing orders to the depots and their impact on carryover. We also discussed and obtained documentation on the actions the Army is taking to better manage and reduce carryover.

We obtained the financial and logistical data in this report from official budget documents and the Army's logistical system. To assess the reliability of the data, we (1) reviewed and analyzed the factors used in calculating carryover for the completeness of the elements included in the calculation, (2) interviewed Army officials knowledgeable about the carryover data, (3) reviewed GAO reports on depot maintenance activities, and (4) reviewed customer orders submitted to Industrial Operations to determine whether they were adequately supported by documentation. In reviewing these orders, we obtained the status of the carryover at the end of the fiscal year. We also reviewed the Commander's Critical Item Reports for fiscal years 2011 and 2012 that provide information on inventory items (spare parts) needed by the depots. In reviewing the reports, we determined whether needed inventory items were associated with customer orders that had carryover for the workloads that we reviewed. On the basis of procedures performed, we have concluded that these data were sufficiently reliable for the purposes of this report. We performed our work at the headquarters of the OUSD (Comptroller), the Office of the Assistant Secretary of the Army (Acquisition, Logistics and Technology), and the Office of the Assistant Secretary of the Army (Financial Management and Comptroller), Washington, D.C.; AMC, Huntsville, Alabama; the Aviation and Missile Command LCMC, Huntsville, Alabama; the Tank, Automotive and Armaments Command LCMC, Warren, Michigan; the Anniston Army

Depot, Anniston, Alabama; the Corpus Christi Army Depot, Corpus Christi, Texas; the Letterkenny Army Depot, Chambersburg, Pennsylvania; the Red River Army Depot, Texarkana, Texas; and the Office of the Assistant Secretary of the Army (Acquisition, Logistics and Technology) at Huntsville, Alabama, and Warren, Michigan.

We conducted this performance audit from May 2012 to June 2013 in accordance with generally accepted government auditing standards. Those standards require that we plan and perform the audit to obtain sufficient, appropriate evidence to provide a reasonable basis for our findings and conclusions based on our audit objectives. We believe that the evidence obtained provides a reasonable basis for our findings and conclusions based on our audit objectives.

Appendix II: Comments from the Department of Defense

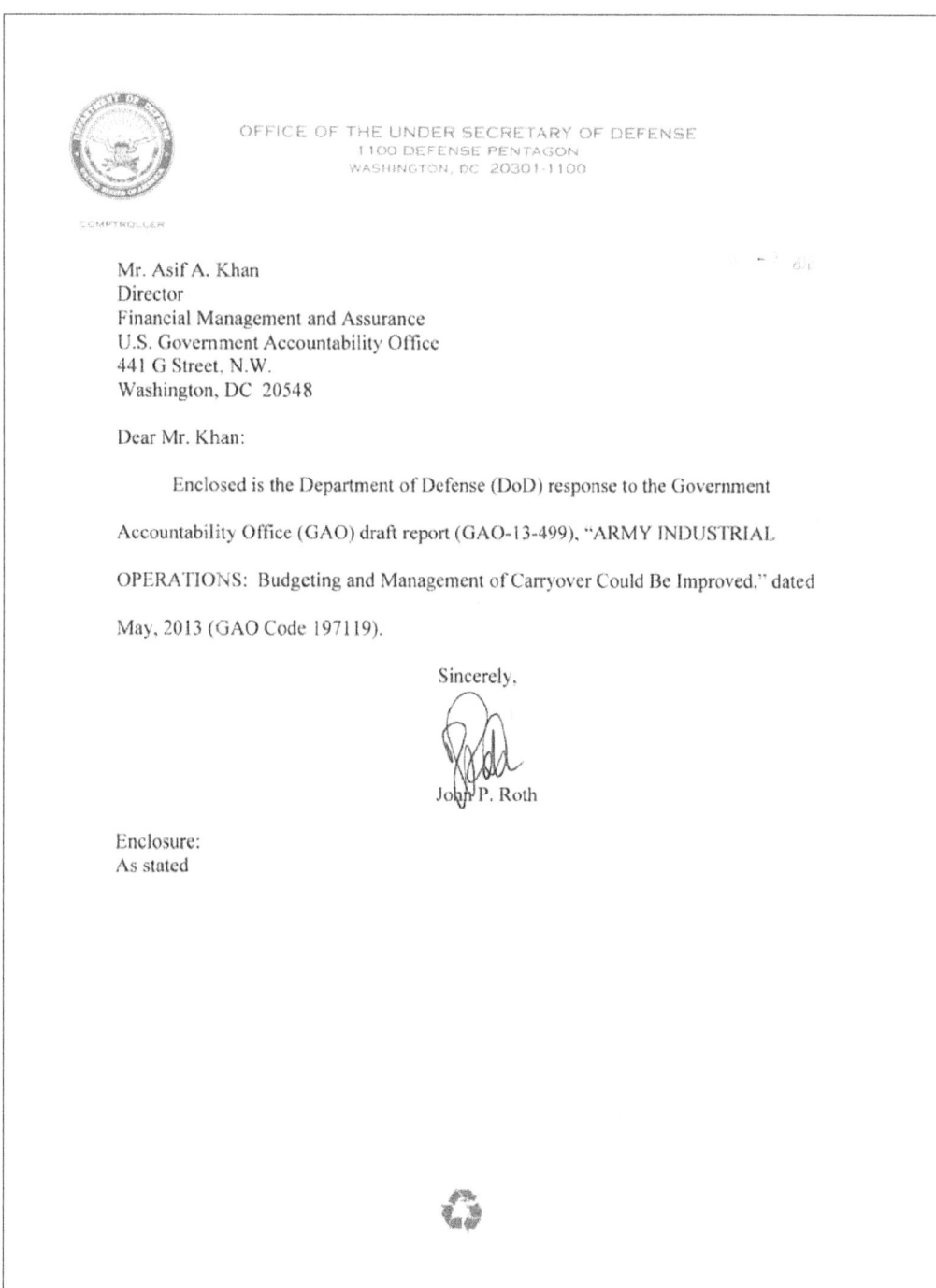

OFFICE OF THE UNDER SECRETARY OF DEFENSE
1100 DEFENSE PENTAGON
WASHINGTON, DC 20301-1100

COMPTROLLER

Mr. Asif A. Khan
Director
Financial Management and Assurance
U.S. Government Accountability Office
441 G Street, N.W.
Washington, DC 20548

Dear Mr. Khan:

Enclosed is the Department of Defense (DoD) response to the Government

Accountability Office (GAO) draft report (GAO-13-499), "ARMY INDUSTRIAL

OPERATIONS: Budgeting and Management of Carryover Could Be Improved," dated

May, 2013 (GAO Code 197119).

Sincerely,

John P. Roth

Enclosure:
As stated

GAO DRAFT REPORT DATED MAY 13, 2013
GAO-13-499 (GAO CODE 197119)

"ARMY INDUSTRIAL OPERATIONS: BUDGETING AND MANAGEMENT OF
CARRYOVER COULD BE IMPROVED"

DEPARTMENT OF DEFENSE COMMENTS
TO THE GAO RECOMMENDATION

RECOMMENDATION 1: The GAO recommends that the Secretary of Defense direct the Secretary of the Army to issue the planned working group policy memos and establish a timetable for implementing these actions on improving the management of carryover.

DoD RESPONSE: Concur. The Army is already preparing to issue, by the end of FY 2013, two policy memorandums with actions therein to be implemented by the beginning of second quarter FY 2014. This is as a result of the working group recommendations coordinated with the Office of the Secretary of Defense (OSD). One memorandum will address the responsibilities and criteria of the organic industrial base activities to accept new orders, whether budgeted or unbudgeted. The other memorandum will specifically address new procurement-funded orders to better align the work to customer delivery schedules.

RECOMMENDATION 2: The GAO recommends that the Secretary of Defense direct the Secretary of the Army to implement the working group's planned actions to improve the budgeting for new orders to be received by Army Industrial Operations.

DoD RESPONSE: Concur. As coordinated with the OSD, the Army has implemented the working group plan to improve budgeting for new orders. The Army continues to hold senior-level quarterly meetings to review Army Industrial Operations (IO) carryover, orders, and revenue status. The Army Materiel Command, the Life Cycle Management Commands, and the Army IO activities are committed to coordinating with customers throughout the budget and requirements process to ensure the most current workload data is identified. Additionally, the Army's FY 2014 Budget Guidance included direction for program managers to identify planned depot workload clearly in procurement budgets beginning in the FY 2014 President's Budget cycle. The same direction will be included in subsequent budget cycle guidance.

RECOMMENDATION 3: The GAO recommends that the Secretary of Defense direct the Secretary of the Army to establish procedures to include required steps to be followed by Army Industrial Operations activities in evaluating orders received from customers to ensure that the activities have resources (such as parts and materials, skilled labor, tools, equipment, technical data, and funding) to perform the work.

DoD RESPONSE: Concur. As coordinated with the OSD, the Army is already in the process of establishing procedures to implement the policy memorandum on the acceptance of new orders. By the beginning of second quarter of FY 2014, Army IO activities will use the procedures to determine acceptance of new orders. Acceptance of new orders will be based on the available resources such as parts and materials, skilled labor, tools, equipment, technical data, and funding to perform the work.

Appendix III: GAO Contact and Staff Acknowledgments

GAO Contact

Asif A. Khan, (202) 512-9869 or khana@gao.gov

Staff Acknowledgments

In addition to the contact named above, Greg Pugnetti (Assistant Director), Steve Donahue, Keith McDaniel, and Hal Santarelli made key contributions to this report.

Please Print on Recycled Paper.